Dear Suicide,

DeVaunier' Cannon

outskirts press

Wow! It's finally finished. I am so thankful. Before I do anything, I just have to give ALL glory to God for blessing me with the vision and wisdom for Dear Suicide, to my Lord and Savior Jesus Christ, and the Holy Spirit, for leading and guiding me along this journey. I am forever grateful for the gift that You have given me to share with Your world.

I have to give a quick shout out to all of my people who supported me. My parents, Dino and Daphne Cannon, who birthed me, loved me, and always let me know that I could do anything through Christ! My sisters Desiree', Daeja, DeJonae, and Traecia who have all inspired me in different ways to be the best me that I can be unapologetically, believed in me when I did not believe in myself, and consistently encouraged me. To my FIVE, Brya, Jasmine, Jasmine, and Lenette, man these women right here, there is no greater examples of friends than them, from helping with research, to staying on my neck to make sure I got everything complete. I thank God for each and every one of you, and I do not know who or where I would be if I did not have you all in my corner.

Lastly, I want to thank my little big brother Dino. Not only was he my very best friend, but he was also my calm in any storm. He is one of my whys. He is one of the main reasons that this book has come to life. Thank you brother for being a comfort, for giving me some of the best laughs of my life, and for loving me with a love that couldn't fade past your death. Until we meet again in Heaven, I LOVE YOU.

John 15:13 NLT
"There is no greater love than to lay down one's life for one's friends."

Table of Contents

Foreword

"Dear Suicide," is no ordinary book. Throughout the duration of this read, there will be various activities that you will be asked to participate in. Although participation is not required, it would be beneficial for you to take part in the journals and questionnaire.

Attempting to write this book has been one of the most challenging experiences that I have ever had. It has caused me to go back to a time in my life that I wish I could forget. But then I remember that every experience is not in vain. I believe that God allowed me to go through certain situations that give me the ability to relate and empathize with others who have gone through, or are currently going through suicidal ideation.

One thing that I ask, is that you leave your expectations of what you think this "should be", at the front cover. Expectations, at times, can ruin a good thing. Instead of letting that happen, just take this time to really feel what you are reading. Whatever emotions you may feel, give yourself permission and the opportunity to feel them without any barriers. I pray that this book provides healing, insight, and understanding for each and every one of you who read it.

Now that all of the formalities are out of the way, are y'all ready to get real? When I say get real, I simply mean to be honest. I hope so. Please be aware that this book has content that may not be appropriate for children under 10 years old. Suicide is a complicated and sensitive subject. Therefore, I request that you act responsibly and guide your loved ones as they read the book if they are not capable of understanding on their own. THANK YOU for all of the support and I KNOW that you will be blessed after completion.

CHAPTER 1

Dear Suicide,

Dear Suicide,

I am not really sure what you are, or what you want from me, but I think I want to be friends with you. Right now, it seems like you are the only one who truly understands me. You see that I am lonely. You see that I have come to my wits end.

Why can't other people recognize the way that I am feeling? Why isn't there anyone who can help me? What? What did you just say? You want me to commit to you? I heard you were serious, so I am not too sure that I want to commit to you just yet. Can I have some time to think about it? No? What's the rush on commitment anyways? You said you will be around anytime I start to feel any emotions that are uncomfortable. Feelings of depression, anger, disappointment, low self-esteem, self-hatred, hatred of others, and any other characteristics of hopelessness. I appreciate the offer, but maybe we can try again another time.

With Love,

-Your soon to be friend

HEY! YOU! YES, I am talking about you! Why are you reading my life? Are you sure you want to go into a place that is so deep, it causes people young and old to take their lives daily? Are you ready for truths that will be revealed? Are you sure you want to go through this journey to see where it takes you? If your answer is no to any of these questions, you might want to go ahead and close the book here. If you are looking for a "feel good" story, again, you may want to close the book now and NEVER look back.

This book was not designed to be a fairytale of a person experiencing a rough situation and then ending up on top of the world. This book is designed to shed light on a plague that is terrorizing our world. To educate children, teenagers, and adults, on where suicidal ideation may come from and how to prevent losing your loved one or even someone you barely know from making a decision that will cost them everything. Still think you want to continue reading? Sigh, alright… shaking my head… DON'T SAY I DIDN'T WARN YOU!

To date, there are many reasons why people choose to commit suicide. When you see the word suicide, what are the first words to pop into your head? Sadness. Depression. Loneliness. Selfishness. Abuse. Rape. Bullying. Death. Maybe your mind went to phrases instead of single words, such as; giving up, cop out, or weak minded.

Oftentimes we want to ask the question "why?". Why would they want to harm themselves? Why didn't they tell someone? Why did they do this to their family and friends? WHY??…Why is not always the question that needs an answer. Sometimes people do not understand why they think, feel, or behave the way in which they do. It can be troublesome to pinpoint the one or even multiple things that may trigger an attempt or thought of suicide.

So, if we don't ask why, what do we ask? Great question! Try asking how or what. How can we help you in this moment? What can we do right now to keep you safe? This aids in keeping the focus on the present instead of what occurred in the past, which may be one of the many reasons that they want to hurt themselves in the first place.

Take a few moments to think about what you just read. What thoughts went through your mind as you were reading? What are some of the words or phrases that come to mind when you see the word suicide? Can you identify with the person writing the letter? In what way? If not, what did you find to be different? Any emotions that you experienced during this chapter, make yourself aware of them through writing.

CHAPTER 2

Answer this!

To you my next conquest,

I am so glad you found me. I wasn't sure if you would ever get this far. I see that life is getting hard. You know, you really shouldn't have to deal with everything you are going through. You are such a good person. You haven't done much wrong. So why are YOU out of all people going through this hardship? You don't deserve this.

Honestly, if you just die, you won't have to worry about anything. Peace is surely to come soon after. Life is overrated anyways. That is why it is important for you to go ahead and kill yourself. I hate seeing you in so much pain. Stop stalling and DO IT. I will be waiting for you on the other side. You won't regret it, haha because even if you did, it would be too late.

Unlike the other people in your life, I will always be here, lingering around, and waiting for you to call on me. Remember that. I hope you decide to come with me. I won't let you down. But by the way things are happening now, I know I will be hearing from you soon. I wouldn't recommend this, butttt, if you want to start off slow to get your feet wet before the big commitment, you can start off with harming yourself. Because I am so nice, I will throw out a few suggestions on how. You can cut yourself (anywhere), burn yourself (anywhere), doing drugs is always a good one, and just engaging in any type of risky behavior will do. The self-harming, will help you move closer to me. Feeling the physical pain is better than dealing with the emotional stuff. I mean, you don't have to do it, it's just a suggestion.

Sincerely,

-Your friend suicide

Have you ever or are you currently self-harming? Yes or No
If yes, how do you self-harm? How often? How does it make you feel?

Have you ever thought about committing suicide? Yes or No
Have you ever attempted suicide? Yes or No
If yes, how did you attempt? How many attempts? How you felt after the attempt(s)? Are you still considering suicide at this time?

When answering these questions, if you answered yes, but do not think that you are at risk of harming yourself, please seek support from family, friends, or a professional. If you feel that you are currently at risk of killing yourself please do not hesitate to call this hotline 1-800-273-8255 or 9-1-1 if you are in more immediate danger. If you answered no to all three questions honestly, please proceed to the next chapter.

CHAPTER 3

Hopelessness

Dear Suicide,

I am exhausted. When is enough, enough? Why is this happening to me? You are right, I don't deserve this. Do you know how it feels to try and try and still fail? Do you understand what life is like when darkness surrounds you and there is no happiness to be found? Can you imagine having NO ONE? No one to lean on, to talk to, or just have someone who cares. That is how I feel right now.

Nothing is changing. I have given it more than enough time to see what would change. Things are only getting worse. I can tell that I have lost hope. I do not want to live. Life has a way of breaking you, and finally, I am broken. My family and friends will live better lives now that they do not have to be brought down by my negativity. The people who treat me badly won't be able to hurt me anymore. There won't be anything left that can cause me stress, anger, or sadness. I would rather be dead right now. There is no future for me. It won't matter anyhow. People do not notice me, so they will not miss me when I'm gone. I have already thought of how

I could kill myself. Waiting any longer to do it, is not an option anymore. Thanks for being here for me. Hopefully I will be dead before the end of this letter...................

My first suicide attempt was on June 15, 2012. I went through a traumatic event that altered my life course. Witnessing the murder of my little brother caused me to go into a brief psychotic state. I was manic. The doctors told my sisters, my brother's very best friends, and I that he passed away from the gunshot wound inflicted by a complete stranger. We all lost it.

Before I knew it, I had a telephone cord wrapped around my neck. I could feel myself drifting off into the "light". It wasn't until I was almost unconscious that I realized two police officers attempting to remove the cord from my death grip. I WAS PISSED! I wanted to die, and they were trying to keep me alive. Why? Why would they take that moment away from me? It was my decision to make. I was so close, I could feel death. I wanted to be dead.

To be honest, that was not the first time I have contemplated suicide, and it definitely wouldn't be the last. There have been multiple occurrences in my life when I just knew that everything and everyone would be better off without me. I've encountered so many negative things, that I felt I would never get past. I WAS HOPELESS.

Every emotion that we feel is first generated by a thought. Thinking negatively or positively influences the way we feel and behave. If this is in fact true, why can't people just change their thoughts to positive so that life will appear better? That only makes sense. Right?

Question. Have you ever had an experience that left you in a pool of negativity that you could not seem to climb out of? Or has life been unfair and it seems as if nothing will ever go your way? Our life situations shape the way we perceive life to be. If we believe that we have gone through more bad than good, our outlook will exhibit that.

Naturally, it is easier to develop a pessimism about life and the world around us. The impact of thinking in a negative manner, is in the negative emotions and behaviors (actions) that follow it. It can be a vicious cycle. You start with a negative thought that leads to a negative emotion, which creates negative behaviors that produce even more negative thoughts. This cycle can develop in any order.

Eventually, you become accustomed to thinking negatively. When you come across any circumstances that may be slightly uncomfortable, those negative thoughts are solidified. The opinion that life sucks is no longer just an opinion, but is now a proven fact based upon your experiences.

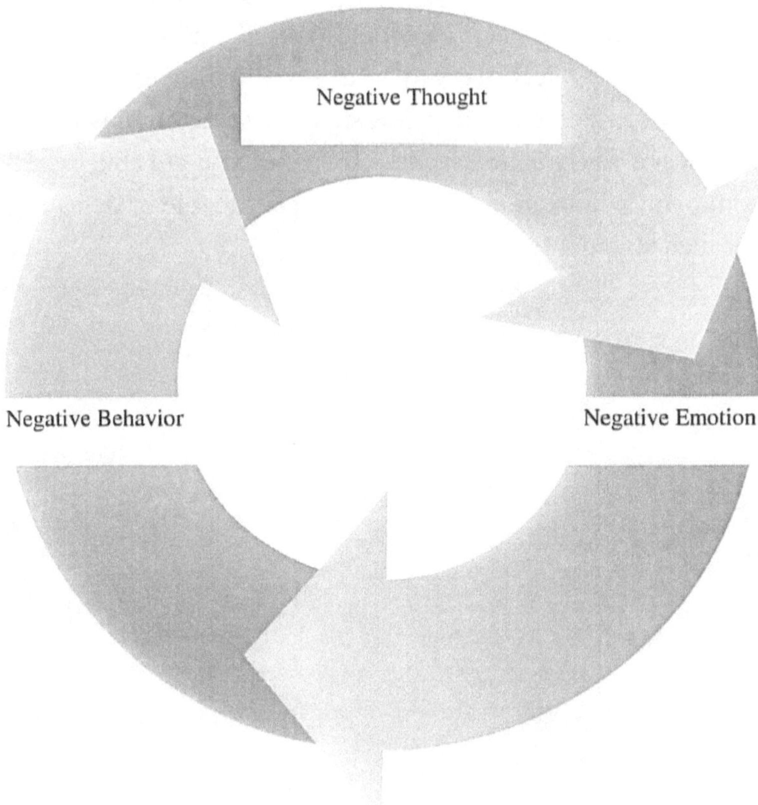

Whenever you are hopeless, a common symptom of depression, it is extremely difficult to want to be positive and do positive things. I know, I've been there. There is low motivation and a lack of energy to engage in any activities that could build positive results. Challenging negative thought processes take a lot of hard work. You literally have to work on combating the thoughts daily. It can be as simple as altering the thought of "today is a terrible day", to "that moment of the day was not great, but I will not let it ruin the rest of my day. It will get better".

I am not saying that it is unacceptable to acknowledge the "bad" thoughts or events. Dwelling on them is what aids in the continuance of hopelessness and the negative thought process cycle. Understand that every moment that you have breath in your lungs, you have another opportunity for greater to come. Every day that you wake up is a blessing. It may not feel that way in this moment, and that is alright. Coming out of a depressive, hopeless state is not easy and is very rarely a quick process. There is no easy fix. But once you are able to get over this hump, you will be grateful that you were capable of defeating this demon called suicidal ideation.

Have you ever felt hopeless? Are you hopeless now? Do you know what occurred that brought on the hopeless feelings? How long would you say the feeling of hopelessness lasts? Is there anything that may cause you to have some hope? What would that be? What would need to change in order for you to have hope and want to live? If you are not the suicidal person, have you ever seen or been around someone who has been hopeless? Were you able to recognize what hopelessness looked like? What were some of the signs?

CHAPTER 4

WHO? Me? You? Them?

Dear friend,

I see that you attempted to get to me. What happened? You can't even do this right. UGH! Since you couldn't complete the task, now you have to worry about what other people are going to think and say about you. People were counting on you to do this, I was counting on you. Now you have to explain to everyone what is going on. They are going to call you crazy. No one is going to want to be around you now. Is that what you want? It must be! Guess you didn't try hard enough. SMH! I'm disappointed. You must like to be in pain.

No worries, you can always try again. But remember, the longer you stay without attempting, the more guilt and shame you will feel. I know you don't want that. So, go ahead and try again until you succeed. I'm rushing you now! The pressure is on! I will be waiting for you.

-Suicide

Anyone can be at risk. There is not a specific person or personality type that excludes you from being an individual that attempts suicide or self-harm. However, statistics show individuals who are more at risk than others based upon their age, gender, sexual orientation, risky behavior patterns, etc. Risky behavior such as doing drugs, drinking and driving, and unprotected sexual encounters, increase the likelihood of suicide because they can ultimately lead to death or harm to oneself. They can be seen as intentional self-harm tactics, since the individual is actively making the decision to partake in the behaviors. Below are bullet points that describe various risk factors of people who are more likely to attempt suicide. These include but are not limited to:

- Older Americans over 45 years old.
- Adolescents and young adults between the ages of 15-24.
- Men across various ages.
- Individuals who have prior attempts or engage in self-harm or self-injury.
- People with medical conditions/illnesses, mental health disorders, and substance use disorders.
- Any preexisting trauma: physical, emotional, and/or sexual abuse.
- Being exposed to others' suicidal behavior.
- Major life changes or loss (grief): financial stress, relationships, rejection, death, becoming homeless, etc.
- Members of the military or veterans.
- Individuals who are gay, lesbian, and or transgender.

Being able to recognize warning signs is imperative. Noticing the behaviors of someone who may be thinking of harming themselves can literally mean life or death. Not saying that if you don't catch it, it is your fault. Let's be clear on that. No one is at fault when someone decides to take their life. Nevertheless, the bullet points below describe warning signs that may be seen in individuals who might be thinking about attempting suicide. These include but are not limited to:

- Unbearable feelings which are marked by unmanageable feelings of hopelessness, despair, self-doubt, guilt, shame, etc.
- Making final plans such as; giving away valuables, creating wills, getting life insurance, speaking about what others will do after they are "gone".
- Rehearsing suicide by thinking, researching, and planning a way to kill themselves.
- Purchasing or storing weapons and or holding on to large amounts of medication (50% of deaths are by firearms).
- Drug and Alcohol use and abuse, which may lead to impulsive behavior.
- Isolation or withdrawal from others like family and or friends.
- A sudden sense of calm, meaning their mood may swing from extremely sad to happy or peace, which can mean they decided on a plan.
- Talking about wanting to die or being a burden to others.

If you see, feel, or hear anything that causes you to question whether someone that you are in contact with is contemplating suicide, ask them directly. Asking someone about their suicidal ideation does not place the thoughts into their head about suicide if they haven't had them before. It does not expedite the process of them attempting. You do not have to be an expert to help save someone from hurting themselves. Do not wait, be persistent, and allow the person to talk freely. Give yourself plenty of time to speak about this matter with the individual. This is not a conversation that can be rushed. If you are not comfortable with asking the person directly, ask someone else who can do it for you.

Do you fit in any of the risk factor categories? Which ones? What about the warning signs? Which ones have you displayed? What did you learn that you didn't know before? Is there anything that you disagree with? Are there any risk factors or warning signs that caught your attention? Do you think it would be a challenge to talk about suicide with someone that you love or someone that you barely know? Why or why not? Any additional thoughts? Feelings?

CHAPTER 5

SAFETY First

Dear Suicide,

It is starting to seem as though anything I do to try to bring harm to myself fails. There is not too much more that I can try to do to get to you. I am not understanding the reason why I am unable to do what so many others have accomplished. What is the reason behind all of this? Is there a reason? Why am I STILL here? I have practically been begging to die. Since my last attempt, I have become even more depressed. You never told me that if I tried and failed that I would feel worse.

Dying is all that I think about, and I am tired of feeling this way. I am tired of living this way. Obviously, I'm not meant to meet you. I know you are disappointed. Believe me, I am too. So what is next? Where do I go from here? How do I deal with having to be here on this earth and I don't want to? Any suggestions?

I know you are all about death, but dying is not appearing to be an option for me. If you do not come up with anything, I promise this will be my last letter to you. I have been relying on you so heavily and all you have done is lied and tricked me.

Everything that you have whispered to me, I have done, and where did that get me? HUH? NOWHERE!

YOU have caused me more pain than my actual situation. YOU say that you are the solution, but you have not solved one of my problems. Honestly, you have not been helpful thus far, so why would you start now? Now that I am thinking about it, I actually don't want your feedback. I don't want any of your "so called" help. I would rather do this on my own. I will be better off that way. So if I haven't made myself clear, DON'T ever talk to me again. LEAVE ME ALONE. I AM NOT YOUR FRIEND.

-Me

After a suicide attempt, individuals can have feelings of failure, confusion, anger, helplessness, and/or hopelessness. Some dive deeper into depression, which can open the door for continued self-harm or other suicide attempts. Others may decide that they will live until they pass naturally. Whichever a person chooses, it is imperative to ensure that they have a plan set that will help keep them safe.

In this chapter, I am going to walk you through an outline of a safety plan that can be used for you or someone else who may need it. Regardless who the plan is for, please try to complete it with another person present. The present party should be someone that you trust. I ask that it be done with support in order to ensure that at least one person knows about your plan, and will be able to help you carry out the plan, whenever you have thoughts of suicide.

When creating the safety plan, you want to have a clear mindset. By that, I mean that you want to do it when you are not feeling suicidal or any other negative emotions. Build the plan when you are in a good headspace so that you will be able to come up with plans that will be effective. Remember that honesty is the best policy. Be honest with yourself, be honest with your support. Specificity is also crucial in completing this process.

Step 1 of the safety plan begins with thoughts about when you would find it necessary to refer or look back at your plan. Think of times or a time when you have felt suicidal. What kind of thoughts were going through your mind? What were your feelings about yourself? The world around you? Was there a specific event that led to the suicidal thoughts? How can you tell that you are becoming suicidal? Do you have racing thoughts? Do you begin to engage in risky behavior? Do you start to self-harm? Questions such as these encompass what we call warning signs. Knowing your warning signs will help you pick up on the tell tell signs that you may be having suicidal ideation.

Step 2 of the plan allows you to view different ways to regulate yourself. How can you talk yourself "off of the ledge"? What can you do to calm yourself down? What can you use to distract you from the blaring thoughts of suicide or any other negative thoughts? What will keep you safe in THIS moment? This step will be introduced in the plan as coping skills.

Step 3 highlights reasons for living. Is there anything in your life that makes it bearable? Do you have any goals? Can you identify one person or people that will be affected by your death? What can you and only you offer to this world by choosing life? If you do not have answers to these questions, that is alright. That is why your support is there. They will aid you in understanding your impact and help you come up with reasons to live.

Step 4 asks you to acknowledge who your support is. Who can you call when you are dealing with overwhelming thoughts that you cannot handle on your own? Do you trust that person enough to share your thought processes? Do they help you feel safe? Are they easy to talk to? Are they understanding? Listing at least three individuals is good, but if you have more please add them as well. If you do not have three that is fine, I just want to be sure that you have at least one person who can support you. Please do not be one of those people who believe they can do it alone. Support is vital in the changing process. So if you don't have one person, do your best to connect with others. You never know how just asking a random person to help you with this can be life changing. You will need their name and a working phone number. Having their address would be a plus, but if you do not have that much, don't worry.

Step 5 lists any professionals that you see, that would be helpful during this time. Professionals such as psychiatrist, therapist, primary care physicians, etc. Please contact them if you have them.

Step 6 involves creating a safe environment for yourself. Are there any weapons that you may have access to? Do you own or have access to any lethal medications? Is there anything that you may think that you would harm yourself with? If you answer yes to any of the above questions, be sure to get rid of them if possible or move them to a place that is very difficult to access. Making things less accessible, will slow you down and hopefully calm you down before you get to the point of self-harm.

Step 7 helps you to have an additional plan if steps 1-6 do not decrease your suicidal ideation, and you still feel as though you cannot keep yourself safe. For instance; will you call the suicide hotline, call 9-1-1, can you have your support drive you to the nearest hospital, can you transport yourself to the hospital safely, etc.

Step 8 asks you to establish a pledge or vow to yourself. In your own words, promise yourself that you will do everything in your power to live. Even when you are pushed to the edge or ready to give up. In this pledge, remind yourself why you deserve to give yourself another chance at life.

Take your time on this plan, there is literally no rush! Also this plan can be fluid, so as you grow and change, your plan can change as well! It is not set in stone!

Step 1: How do I know that I am feeling suicidal? What are my warning signs?

1.	
2.	
3.	
4.	

Step 2: How can I calm myself down? What coping skills work for me?

1.	
2.	
3.	
4.	

Step 3: What makes life worth living? Do I have any goals?

1.	
2.	
3.	
4.	

Step 4: Who can I call when I need support? What are their phone numbers/addresses?

Name:	Phone Number:	Address
1.		
2.		
3.		
4.		

Step 5: Do you have any professionals that you can contact?

Name:	Phone Number
1.	
2.	
3.	

Step 6: Is your environment safe? Are there any weapons/medications that can cause bodily injury?

1.
2.
3.
4.

Step 7: Still not safe? What is your plan?

1. Call 9-1-1
2. Call the Suicide Hotline- 1-800-273-8255
3.
4.

Step 8: I pledge that when I begin to feel suicidal I will...

CHAPTER 6

Help me, Help you

Dear Loved One,

I didn't have a clue that you were feeling this way. Why didn't you tell me? I know that you were going through an extremely tough time, but you know that you can talk to me about any-thing. I was terrified when I found you lying there almost lifeless. What would I have done if you would have died? How would I be able to live with myself knowing that I could have done more? What could I have done differently to keep you from trying to kill yourself? I never want this to happen again. Tell me how to help you. Tell me what you need. I will do whatever it takes to keep you here. Please don't leave me. This world needs you. I need you! Please....

With love,

-Someone who cares

One thing that I am aware of is that sometimes we don't know what to do. We don't know what to say that will be helpful or keep our loved ones safe. Here are few tips that you can use to support the suicidal person:

- Let them know that you are worried about them and try to understand their thoughts and feelings.
- Be specific with them about what actions or events cause you to worry.
- If they feel guilty about anything, attempt to help them overcome that guilt. Guilt is treatable. We all make mistakes. It is not about what you have done, but what you will do differently now that you know you made a mistake. How will you use your new knowledge to help someone else?
- As a support it is NOT your responsibility to make the person better. Time and again, we find ourselves wanting to fix problems. Please understand that it is not your issue to fix. All you are there to do is continue to encourage them while also trying to obtain professional help for them.
- When or if the individual has to be hospitalized for any reason pertaining to suicide or self-harm, stay in contact with them. You can make visits or calls to the hospital to check in with them. To remove stress, you may offer to help them with any tasks they may have waiting for them upon their return home.
- Continue to be there for them by helping them remain in treatment via continuing care with a psychiatrist, therapist, or support group.

If a person is threatening to harm themselves in that moment:

- Emphasize that there is hope and help that can be provided.
- ALWAYS take the threat seriously.
- Do not attempt to handle the situation by yourself. Bring other people to help you.
- Be understanding, state your concerns, and do not be judgmental.

- DO NOT leave the person by themselves until they are in the care of professionals such as; hospital staff, therapist, psychiatrists, etc.

Unfortunately, for some of you, your loved one actually completed suicide. There are no words to express my condolences for you and the others that have been affected by the loss you experienced. I cannot imagine the feelings that you have currently or have had at the time of the passing. A major suggestion I have for you is to not place blame. Not on yourself, not on others. Thinking about the "what ifs", "what you could have done", and "why didn'ts" only bring about unwarranted guilt. IT IS NOT ANYONE'S FAULT. I repeat, IT IS NOT ANYONE'S FAULT! Suicide is the ultimate decision a person can make. Notice I said decision. No one can make another person harm themselves. It is a choice that only the person considering it can make. So please do not take on being the reason for them passing.

Dealing with the aftermath of suicide is rough. Be sure to allow yourself to grieve. Grief has many stages and it does not look the same for everyone. It is perfectly normal to feel emotions like anger, confusion, sadness, and guilt. You may also experience physical aches and pains, and changes in eating or sleeping patterns. These are normal reactions.

If you feel overwhelmed, be sure to find support of your own. Talk to others about your experience and find a support group. Do not be afraid to consult with a professional about what you are going through, especially if you begin to have thoughts of suicide. Get help immediately. Being honest about how you feel and what you went through can be helpful for you and others who may be going through the same thing.

Time to be mindful. Notice your thoughts and feelings about the entire chapter. Write it out. Whatever it was, whether positive or negative, happy or sad. It is important to be able to be mindful and recognize the way this topic makes you think and feel.

CHAPTER 7

Take Care

Dear Support,

Thank you. Thank you for having the strength to help. Thank you for caring. I might not have told you at the time, but you have made such an impact by simply being there. Your presence alone, made the difference. This must have been extremely challenging for you to watch me go from bad to worse. To have to listen to my pain and talk me down. I never meant to involve you. I don't know what I would do if the roles were reversed. You need to know that you have helped keep me alive. Thank you for helping me find that little glimmer of light. For opening that door of hope. Showing me all the while how important I am and why I need to fight for my life.

Now I am concerned about you. I notice that you seem fatigued. You are not resting well and forgetting to eat. You are always worried about me. You don't do anything to relax. You don't do anything for yourself anymore. I need you to take care of you now. I don't want you to have a breakdown because of me. I promise you that I will take care of myself, so that you can take care of you. Get some rest. I will be fine. I Love You.

-Me

Being a support of any kind is hard. It can be emotionally, physically, and mentally draining. Caring for yourself is more than enough to keep you busy. Adding on to that by having to be responsible for an actively or passively suicidal person can cause emotional distress and fatigue. Emotional distress can be displayed through physical symptoms of aches and pains. This distress can also be expressed through emotional, behavioral, and cognitive symptoms.

Emotional symptoms involve moodiness, agitation, anxiety, feelings of being overwhelmed, depression, and overall unhappiness. Behavioral symptoms may include altered eat and sleep routines, isolation, and or using alcohol or drugs to "take your mind off of things". Cognitive symptoms that could be experienced are inability to concentrate, negative thinking, excessive worrying, or memory problems.

It is important to recognize these symptoms. If it is found that you are having any of these symptoms frequently, attempt to connect with others. Begin talking through some of what you are feeling. To relieve stress, get active. Start going for walks, or exercising, not just when you are having these symptoms, but make it into a habit. If not daily, at least a few days out of the week. Being active aids in removing toxins out of the body, which ultimately will help you feel better.

Finding various calming agents will reduce symptoms of emotional distress. Anything that deals with the five senses that relaxes you, use it. Is there a smell, taste, something that you hear, something that you feel, or something that you may see that produces a calming effect? Now I am not encouraging anything illegal, so please do not take that out of context. I mean things like fragrances, stress balls, listening to rain or the ocean, eating a healthy snack, or looking at a painting. Understanding that you cannot get rid of all your stress, but that you can control what type of effect it has on you, will be helpful in the self-care process. Lastly, being sure to get adequate sleep and eating healthily can affect your mood in a positive or negative way. When you are not eating or resting well, stress can increase, and then you can become emotionally unbalanced and less productive.

It is a beautiful thing to be available to help others when they are having issues. Life becomes troublesome when we attempt to take on others' problems, and are not able to take care of ourselves. From either side, what is your take on self-care for support systems? Do you have any alternative suggestions for yourself or others? Any additional comments or thoughts?

Epilogue

Dear Reader,

I know that reading a book about suicide is not ideal, but I am so thankful that you have made it to the very end. It is my prayer that you have gained either hope for yourself or a better understanding about how suicide can entice and affect people. In my introduction I stated that writing this book has been one of the most arduous tasks that I have completed in my lifetime. Having to relive that part of my life was extremely tough and eye opening. I wanted to be as transparent with you as I could, without making the entire book about my life story, because it is not about me. It is ALL about you! I wanted to be able to help at least one person push through their current situation. I've been there, not once, but multiple times. I wish I could say it would get better right now, or even tomorrow, but for some it does not. For that I am sorry.

I do recognize that when things don't seem to be changing for the better, how hopeless it can make you feel. Do not allow those temporary emotions, to put a premature end to your life. They are temporary. Nothing lasts forever. Weeping may endureth during the night, but joy comes in the morning. You can take that literally or figuratively. Your joyful morning may not actually be the next morning, but it will come in due time! Be patient. Let my book be a constant reminder to you that although it appears that your circumstances will not change, if you do your best to continue to live with purpose, eventually something will change in your favor. Whatever you do, JUST DON'T GIVE UP on yourself. If you allow it, life can be beautiful, even when you are going through your rough patch. Do your best to try to find at least one positive thing you can focus on. If you are having trouble keeping yourself safe, think of every passing second, and promise yourself that you can make it another second, another minute, another hour, another day. It may be a day to day thing. Just continue to tell yourself that YOU CAN do it.

Whether or not you believe it, you DESERVE to live. You owe it to yourself to give you your best shot at life. Speaking from experience, there is always at least one thing that you can offer someone else. If no one else tells you this, I believe in you, I want you to live, I want you to be happy, I want you to grow and help someone else along the way. YOU are Fearfully and Wonderfully made. YOU are NEEDED. YOU are IMPORTANT. YOU are CARED for. YOU are LOVED. YOU ARE A SURVIVOR!

-DeVaunier'

2 Corinthians 4:16-18 NLT

"That is why we never give up. Though our bodies are dying, our spirits are being renewed every day. For our present troubles are small and won't last very long. Yet they produce for us a glory that vastly outweighs them and will last forever! So we don't look at the troubles we can see now; rather, we fix our gaze on things that cannot be seen. For the things we see now will soon be gone, but the things we cannot see will last forever.

As this is the final journal of the book, I would like for you to write about your experience. What have you learned about suicide? What you have learned about yourself? What have you learned about what others may feel that led or is leading them to suicide? Did journaling help you express yourself? Was this book helpful? What has changed in your thought processes? How do you feel now that you have completed the book? How can you help someone else having suicidal ideation?

Again, I thank you all for reading! I will continue to be praying that God moves in a powerful way on your behalf! I Love Y'all!!

If you would like more information on suicide, here are websites that provided some of the information from this book:

- nimh.nih.gov (Suicide in America: Frequently asked questions)
- afsp.org/about-suicide/risk-factors-and-warning-signs/ (American Foundation for Suicide Prevention)
- Samhsa.gov (Populations at Risk for Suicide)
- prb.org/suicides/ (In U.S., Who is at Greatest Risk for Suicides)
- suicidepreventionlifeline.org/wp-content-uploads/2016/08/ brown_stanleysafetyplantemplate.pdf (Patient Safety Plan Template)